When Do
The Good Things
Start?

When Do The Good Things Start?

Abraham J. Twerski, M.D.
PEANUTS® cartoons by Charles M. Schulz

TOPPER BOOKS
AN IMPRINT OF PHAROS BOOKS • A SCRIPPS HOWARD COMPANY
NEW YORK

First published in 1988

Library of Congress Cataloging-in-Publication Data
Twerski, Abraham J.
    When do the good things start?/Abraham J. Twerski;
Peanuts cartoons by Charles M. Schulz.
    p. cm.
    ISBN 0-88687-340-1 (Pharos) : $5.95.
    1. Self-actualization (Psychology)   2. Schulz, Charles M.
Peanuts.   3. Comic books, strips, etc.—Psychological aspects.
I. Title.
BF637.S4T85 1988   87-38081
158'.1—dc19   CIP

Printed in United States of America

📖 TOPPER BOOKS®

An Imprint of Pharos Books
A Scripps Howard Company
200 Park Avenue
New York, NY 10166

10 9 8 7 6 5 4 3 2 1

Cover and text design by Elyse Strongin
Cover airbrush rendering by Carlos Torres

CONTENTS

Why This Book?

Socrates, Aristotle, Freud, Jung, Schulz . . .

Schulz?

Yes, Charles M. Schulz. The man who created Charlie Brown, Lucy, Snoopy, and their friends in the comic strip known the world over as *Peanuts.*®

How did a cartoonist join the company of the world's greatest thinkers, philosophers and psychologists?

Because he has created a comic strip that is a treasury of thought, philosophy and psychology. And if it is true that a picture is worth a thousand words, then Schulz has written more than many of the world's most prolific authors combined.

In Charles M. Schulz we have been blessed with an artist who has an intuitive grasp of human nature and an uncanny ability to condense the most sophisticated psychological concepts into a few cartoon frames. The lovable characters created by Charles Schulz do more than amuse; they depict important psychological principles in a manner so deceptively simple that it masks the force of their impact.

The first application of Schulz's work in my psychiatric practice occurred during a therapy session with an alcoholic. My patient was a very intelligent man whom I had seen on several previous occasions, and who had consistently refused to accept my recommendation for definitive treatment for his alcoholism. Each time we met he denied that he was an alcoholic, and, although on no occasion was he able to deny the alcohol-induced fiasco that had once again brought him to my office, he continued to insist that he could still drink socially. Each time he thought of some new technique whereby he could prevent his drinking from going out of control. Each time I pointed out that his previous efforts had failed, and that his newly devised machination would be no more successful than his previous efforts.

On his last visit I had a sudden inspiration. Sometime earlier I had resolved to make some changes in my lifestyle in order to reduce stress. One of these was to read no work-related material during meals. I, therefore, kept several volumes of light literature in my office for reading during lunch, and these included several volumes of *Peanuts* cartoons.

I remembered how Charlie Brown falls flat on his back each time he tries to kick the football at the beginning of each season. And how every year he rationalizes why *this* year things were going to be different and he was not going to miss the ball. Yet every year the same thing happened. Charlie Brown did not learn from experience.

I told the patient about Charlie Brown's annual ritual and let him read several strips. He laughed heartily, and then to my surprise he said, "That's me, all right."

Charlie Brown had been able to reach this patient in a way that I could not. As a psychiatrist I appeared formidable and threatening. The patient might feel that I was accusing him of not trying hard enough to control his drinking. However, Charlie Brown was innocent and harmless. Charlie Brown gave it his all each time. He really wanted to kick that football with every fiber in his body. It just didn't work.

Schulz's characters don't interpret things for you. They just behave in their own way and allow you to make your own interpretation. Insights that come from the patient rather than from the therapist are always more effective.

When I became medical director of a major psychiatric hospital, I had a section of the bulletin board labeled "Post-Graduate Education" on which I regularly displayed some of Schulz's strips.

More recently I began to wonder if everyone comprehends and appreciates the message of Schulz's *Peanuts*. Certainly the strip is entertaining, but, precisely because of that, most people may think it is *only* entertaining. Because it appears on the comic page with so many other cartoons that are funny and nothing more, perhaps the strip is judged by the company it keeps. This led me to attempt to state more explicitly some of the valuable messages that I saw conveyed by Charlie Brown and his friends.

Are my interpretations valid? Are they what Schulz had in mind when he created the strips? I don't know, nor does it really matter. Reams of essays have been written about the characters in *Hamlet*. Did Shakespeare consciously intend all the meanings others have read into his characters? Again, the question is irrelevant. The characters speak in many different ways to different people. An artist creates with the intuition that inspires him.

So join me, and let us share a variety of human experiences with Charlie Brown and his friends. Who knows? Perhaps we might become just a bit happier and more efficient if we not only listen to, but also *see* what Charles Schulz is telling us.

1. ASSESSING YOURSELF

Let's Begin

Did you ever wonder why it is that with all the efforts to improve mankind throughout the many centuries of recorded history, we nevertheless seem to have made such meager progress?

All the great religious teachings, all the great humanistic movements, all the great philosophies haven't been able to eliminate or reduce bloodshed, greed and hatred. They haven't made the world a better place to live in.

My mother used to say that the problem is that everybody looks after his *own* material needs, but *everyone else's* spiritual needs.

People are full of faults. But I, too, am "people." So it would be best to begin by correcting my own faults.

If we really tried to do this, we might find it to be a full-time job.

We might not even have any time left to look for faults in others.

We could make the world a better place to live, if only we directed our efforts in the right direction: toward ourselves.

Take Inventory!

Taking a personal inventory is an excellent exercise for anyone seeking self-improvement.

It surprises me that some people are frightened of taking a moral inventory. They are afraid they will become profoundly depressed when they discover the many things they have done wrong.

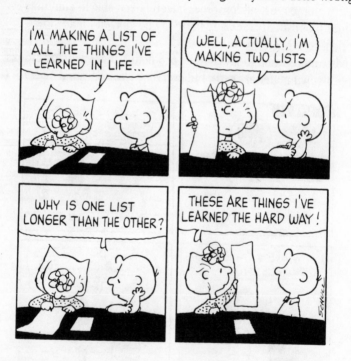

How many valuable lessons can you truthfully list that have come to you easily?

The proverb which says "Experience is a hard teacher but fools will learn in no other way" is wrong. Wise people also learn from experience. Fools are those who do *not* learn from experience.

Make a list of all the things that you recognize you have done wrong. Since you are aware that these were wrong, you are not likely to repeat them. This makes them valuable learning experiences. How can you consider valuable learning experiences to be liabilities? Cheer up. You are not a fool at all, but rather wise enough to learn from your mistakes.

You Are Better Than You Think

M any people do not assess themselves correctly. Some people have inflated self-concepts. They think they are God's gift to the world and believe everyone should recognize and appreciate this.

Others think very little of themselves, and may not be aware of their skills and talents.

A good adjustment to reality requires a correct perception of reality. Delusions about ourselves, whether grandiose or the opposite, are impediments to good adjustment.

Strangely enough, people who think they are smarter than they really are can sometimes (but by no means always) be shaken into reality when things happen that disprove their claim to superiority. But when people are convinced that they are inferior, even absolute proof to the contrary may not alter their negative self-image.

One such woman truly believed she had been elected to Phi Beta Kappa by mistake. Beware of the tendency to underestimate yourself. You are probably a better person than you think you are.

Recognize Your Capabilities

Winners sometimes lose. One of the differences between a winner and a loser is that a winner uses the experience of losing to learn what he does not do well. He then goes on to succeed, using the talents he discerns he *does* have. The loser never learns. He continues to make the same mistakes over and over again.

When every pitch is knocked out of the ballpark, stop pitching. Try playing third base or maybe even selling popcorn.

When reality tries to tell you something, listen!

Don't Be Afraid To Change

Some people who go into therapy make progress until they recognize that treatment will force a change in their behavior. They then become so terrified of the change that they stop the treatment.

Whatever your problem, if it is causing you misery, don't be afraid to change.

Of course, any change can be uncomfortable at first.

So rather than go through the inconvenience of making changes, we may tell ourselves that our difficulties are due to deep-rooted emotional problems. We convince ourselves that there is no point in making any changes in the way we do things because those changes will not affect the deep emotional conflicts that are the source of our difficulties.

The expression on Lucy's face in the last frame can be considered one of triumph. By ascribing her misery to deep-rooted problems, she can avoid the discomfort of changing the way she is living.

People who think this way are often those who never seem to finish their psychotherapy. They can't afford to recover, because giving up their defense of having deep-rooted problems would mean that they would have to change. This is precisely what they wish to avoid by going into psychotherapy in the first place.

Psychotherapy is indeed necessary to solve some problems. But sometimes the best psychotherapy is when we are told to make some changes in our behavior instead of looking for deep-rooted sources for our problems.

It is comfortable to continue to live as we always have done. But if we persevere a bit, the new behavior will soon become the comfortable way, a regular part of life, and we will have eliminated the harmful behavior.

Don't Be Afraid To Try

When you try anything, there are two possibilities: you may succeed or you may fail.

Whereas failure is never pleasant, some defeats are nevertheless tolerable, and so we are willing to take the risk.

Sometimes we will take a risk even when we are virtually certain that we are going to fail, as long as there is at least some slight hope that we might succeed.

Refusing to try something is the result of having absolutely no hope whatever of the possibility of success. Or, even if there were a chance of success, the feeling that failure might result is so devastating that one cannot afford to risk it. If both feelings are present together, trying is virtually out of the question.

Not trying has its consequences over and above ruling out any change of success. It can be depressing and affect your functioning.

2. FACING REALITY

What Is Reality?

Did you ever watch babies put their hands over their eyes to hide from you? Infants think that when they cannot see you, you cannot see them either.

Like other kinds of infantile thinking, this sometimes persists into adult life. There are people who believe that when they are oblivious to something, it simply does not exist.

Don't give yourself a false sense of well-being by making yourself oblivious to reality. If you accept reality for what it is, you can either change it or adapt to it. But you cannot do either if you are not aware that it exists.

Don't Regress

At one time we are each in a mother's womb, fully protected from all external stimuli. Once we leave the womb, we are exposed to all kinds of experiences, some pleasant, some unpleasant.

Although we do not have any conscious memory of this phase of our existence, it seems to have registered somewhere within us, because when unpleasant circumstances arise we are prone to stay in bed, with the covers drawn over our heads, and even curled up in the fetal position.

There is one basic flaw in regressing to the fetal position: the reality is that we no longer have an umbilical cord which will provide us with the necessities of life so that we can survive and grow.

Sometimes people around us will behave like surrogate mothers and allow us to continue our retreat from reality by caring for our needs. But you can't count on this lasting forever.

Don't retreat from reality. It can't work.

Stop The Pity Party

M ost of us can remember how we felt sorry for ourselves when we were children. The bruised forehead or the scraped knee may have gotten us loving care and attention from a devoted parent. We felt hurt, and others cared for us.

This information is stored for years and decades in the memory bank in that personal computer that resides inside our skulls. But the way our brain-computer operates may result in such close association of self-pity with the gratification of being cared for, that we may actually enjoy indulging in self-pity. Some people may go so far as to actually incur pain in order to have something about which to feel sorry for themselves.

Indulging in self-pity is juvenile behavior. It is understandable in small children, but mature adults should try to rectify things that have gone wrong instead of wallowing in misery and pitying themselves for suffering.

Of course, taking corrective action depends on having the confidence that you can do things to extricate yourself from difficulties. If you lack self-confidence, you might opt just to stay where you are and feel sorry for yourself. If a friend or relative drags you out of your misery, you're lucky. But you can't count on it. It is better to get out of it yourself.

Don't Try To Impress People With Make-Believe

When people underestimate themselves, they may think themselves to be unattractive and unlikable. They may then resort to rather desperate measures to impress others with their importance in the hope of attracting attention and possibly even affection.

What these people do not realize is that these efforts are not only futile, they are actually counter-productive. Unaware of their admirable qualities, which could make them likable, they assume attitudes that may actually repel others. Furthermore, they may even begin to believe their own fantasies and lose touch with reality.

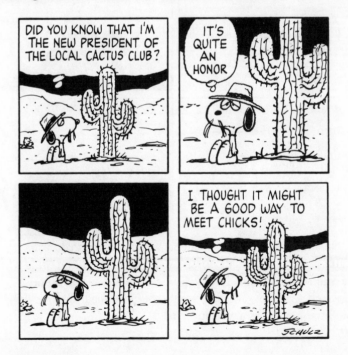

Don't run away from people and reality into a make-believe world.

Adapt To The Present

Why do some people live in the past? Why do others daydream about the future?

This behavior has the same root. Either way you don't have to deal with the present.

The future is very easy to accept. You can fantasize to your heart's content and reality doesn't stand in the way. You *could* win the multi-million dollar lottery. Someone has to win it. Some prince charming or ravishing beauty *could* fall madly in love with you. Stranger things have happened.

Living in the past is a bit more difficult because it may involve distorting things that really did happen. But historians have rewritten history and, if necessary, you can also see your past in a skewed way.

It's that obstinate present that just refuses to yield.

Marcie is in love with Charlie Brown. She tries to let him know that all the time.

But for all her fine qualities Marcie doesn't compare to the little red-haired girl, the great unobtainable love of Charlie Brown's fantasy life. Marcie is the truth of the present, Charlie Brown's reality.

Some people cannot accept the present. The present is far too imperfect. So they do nothing while waiting for their brilliant fantasy future to come to them.

There is nothing wrong with setting your sights high. But you have only one life to live. If you don't accept what reality has to offer, you have only fantasy to support you, which is about as satisfying as the hole in the doughnut in the long run.

Don't Get Lost In Abstractions

*P*hilosophy can be taught in the classroom or be the topic of scholarly discussions, but when people try to use philosophic concepts in coping with everyday life, watch out. In my experience it is often an escape from dealing with reality.

Some people can effectively fool themselves by espousing noble ideals and principles, although in real life they don't give any indication of practicing them.

If you believe in charity, then perform charitable acts. If you believe in equal rights, let's see you accord them to everyone. If you believe in loving your fellow human beings, show me how you manifest that love.

If you want to fool me, go ahead and try. I think I am wise enough not to let myself be fooled. But if you are foolish enough to try and fool yourself, you may also be foolish enough to let yourself be fooled.

Let Your Expectations Be Real

Some people suffer reversals in life. Others complain that their whole life has been one big reversal.

In some of the latter instances, analysis will reveal that these people have had fairly normal circumstances. They have not sustained more losses than the average person, and they have received their fair share of the good things of life.

The problem is that some people have fantasies of what life is supposed to be like, and if the reality does not measure up to their fantasies, they feel cheated. They are rarely satisfied with anything: home, job, marriage, vacation, automobile, children. Nothing can ever measure up to their unrealistic expectations.

Unless you are one of the unfortunate few who have been victims of recurrent disasters, you probably have had some of the good things in life. Your balance, sheet of good things and bad things is probably quite similar to that of most other people.

If you feel you've never been happy, there is a good chance that you haven't really been deprived of happiness, but for some reason you are unable to feel happy for the things that bring some happiness to others.

Don't spend your life in misery because your fantasies are not being fulfilled. Get some competent counseling and bring your expectations into line.

3. SELF-ESTEEM

The Self-Esteem Problem

*E*arly in my psychiatric practice, I came to the conclusion that most emotional problems, except for those that are due to chemical imbalances, are due primarily to people having unwarranted feelings of low self-esteem.

An optimum adjustment to reality requires a correct perception of reality. If one sees the world as different than it really is, the adjustment is certain to be faulty. And if a person sees himself as being less than what he really is, his adjustment is equally certain to be faulty, because, after all, every person is a part of his own reality.

People who are less endowed may not have much difficulty. They may find a niche where they fit nicely and feel quite comfortable. It's when we underestimate ourselves and are not aware of our strengths and assets that we misperceive our own reality, and this misperception can result in a variety of personality problems.

The underestimation of oneself is so prevalent that we can all identify with it in one way or another. This is probably why we all empathize with Charlie Brown, who is a caricature of the person who sees himself as a loser.

But *is* Charlie Brown a loser?

If there were a comic strip character who was physically or mentally handicapped, and was therefore unable to function well, would he be acceptable to us? How amusing would he be? Would you laugh at his clumsiness?

No, Charlie Brown is not an inadequate *person* at all. Charlie Brown is an inadequate *personality*. He sees himself as inadequate, and he therefore functions inadequately, and, consequently, everyone else sees him as being inadequate as well. Charlie Brown personifies the vicious cycle of the person who perceives himself as being negative in every way, and thereby *becomes* that which he thinks himself to be.

We are amused by Charlie Brown because in one way or another he is us. We laugh at him because he reminds us of ourselves, but since he is portrayed in caricature, the exaggeration of our traits sufficiently removes them from ourselves so that we can stand at a distance and allow ourselves to look at them without feeling seriously threatened.

This caricature technique also allows us to laugh at Lucy, because Lucy is the other part of us, the part that knows it all, that can do no wrong. Lucy always has a valid excuse for anything that goes haywire. Just as Charlie Brown sees himself as a total failure, Lucy sees herself as being eminently successful.

Lucy's fielding is no less disastrous than Charlie Brown's pitching, but she can always explain away her failure to catch a ball, while at the same time heaping invective on poor Charlie Brown. Charlie Brown thinks the worst of himself, while Lucy thinks too much of herself. If we examine these traits and how they affect people, we might be able to avoid some of these pitfalls in our own lives.

People with low self-esteem are likely to misinterpret many things in the light of their conviction that they are inadequate, worthless, and unlikable.

Suppose you walk into a room just as another person happens to be leaving. Your coming in and the other person's leaving are totally unrelated.

But if you happen to be a person with low self-esteem, you may think, "He is leaving because he saw me coming. He is just like all the rest. He doesn't like me."

When bad things happen it is a pity, but that is all there is to it. However, if you are prone to self-deprecation, you are apt to interpret everything as an indication of your inadequacy.

If you are really feeling worthless, you may see yourself not only as too inadequate to cope with the world, but as so inadequate that you cannot live with yourself.

Whereas most people can look at both their successes and their failures, people with negative self-images are preoccupied exclusively with their failures, not only the ones that have already happened, but all those that could possibly happen in the future.

People with low self-esteem may be totally oblivious to those things they do that turn out well. In fact, the only thing that they think they can achieve that comes close to success is a failure which is of lesser magnitude.

Some people try to escape from the depression engendered by low self-esteem by making some radical change in their lives. They may change jobs, marry, divorce, or move to another location. However, unless the distortion of their self-image is overcome, they are likely to remain just as depressed after the change of circumstances as before.

When things happen that make you feel bad about yourself, just stop and think. Are these things really a reflection on me? If you could only look at things more objectively, you would find that many things that happen to you are not a measure of your personality at all. You've been allowing your negative feelings to color these incidents. Take off those dark-tinted glasses and let the real world shine through!

In contrast to the character of low self-esteem epitomized by Charlie Brown, Schulz created Lucy, an equally recognizable personality.

These people are apt to be self-righteous and consider themselves the ultimate authorities on everything.

They do not seem to be the least bit bothered by their mistakes, and they have a unique way of seeing even their faults as being virtues.

The truth is that people who behave as though they are God's gift to humanity are also basically people with low self-esteem. They defend themselves against the acceptance of the feeling of low self-esteem by acting superior.

This does not mean that these people think themselves to be inferior and are just putting on a facade of superiority. They actually do believe in their superiority and are not acting at all. They may in fact be excellent people, although probably not as excellent as they think they are. However, this conviction of their superiority is a reaction to an underlying and generally unconscious feeling that they are actually inadequate. Their constant need to criticize and belittle others is a technique to bolster their own self-esteem.

This may sound strange, but look at it this way.

People who really feel adequate and happy within themselves have no need to push other people around or to be critical of them.

People who feel thoroughly adequate can accept criticism and can debate the issues. However, when people who act as though they are superior in reaction to underlying feelings of inferiority are subject to criticism, they cannot stand up to it. They are apt to strike out. They attack other people's personalities rather than deal with issues.

Sometimes a self-confident and assertive person is caught off guard and the underlying feelings of insecurity and the fear of being unloved come through. At such times, this person may be very much like Charlie Brown, so despairing of being loved that he cannot accept love even when it is tendered.

Just as Charlie Brown is unable to accept any positive statements about himself, the Lucy type may also not believe compliments directed to her, in spite of the fact that she frequently indulges in self-adoration.

Of the two types of low self-esteem personalities described, the Charlie Brown type is usually more likable than the Lucy type.

Of course, getting affection because someone feels sorry for you is not ideal, but it's better than what the other type get with their pushiness.

Good friends can and do help us to overcome feelings of low self-esteem by making us aware of our assets.

The problem is learning to differentiate between the honest appraisal of real friends and the casual remarks of acquaintances. Social interchange is not always reliable. Politeness is valued in our culture, and we think that we ought to tell people things that they would like to hear, whether they are true or not.

Hence, when people compliment you, ask yourself, do they really mean it or are they just being polite?

Now, if someone that does *not* like you says something nice about you, *that* can be taken as reliable, and that kind of compliment can, indeed, make you feel better.

4. LOVE AND FRIENDSHIP

Do You Know What Love Is?

Are love and passion identical? Not if we define love as sincere consideration for another person and passion as an appetite we wish to satisfy.

True love is directed toward another person. If necessary we will sacrifice our own comfort to make that other person happier. But passion can be simply selfish gratification. So if what you feel is passion, don't expect to receive love in return.

Do you love someone? Have you told him or her how intense your feelings are? Were you upset by the lack of reciprocation?

How much of what you feel for the other person is true love, and how much is the gratification of your needs by the other person? It is okay to be hungry, and it is okay to feel passion. Just don't mistake either of these two feelings for love.

How much of your own gratification are you willing to sacrifice for the person whom you profess to love?

Do Something About That Lonely Feeling

*L*oneliness is one of the most unpleasant feelings a person can experience.

Sometimes things beyond our control can result in our being lonesome. Friends move to other cities, acquaintances die, and health problems may limit our mobility.

But even when things happen that may bring about loneliness, we do not have to resign ourselves to it.

Making new acquaintances may not be easy. We often think that other people are part of a clique and we would be unwelcome intruders.

Sometimes our sense of pride gets in our way. We may think that if people really want us as friends, then they should initiate the relationship, and if they don't, we remain alone.

Companionship may come easily and develop spontaneously in some stages of life. At other times, it may require effort and its pursuit may be fraught with some disappointments.

But unless you are willing to live with the misery of loneliness, you had better take some constructive action.

Make Yourself Visible

A young woman consulted me because she felt that "Life was passing her by." She longed for male companionship, but no one seemed interested in her.

The woman was quite attractive and had a pleasant personality. Why, then, was she so isolated?

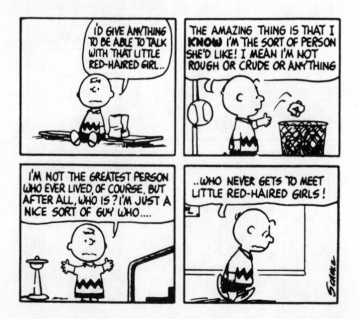

Questioning revealed that she had made herself virtually inaccessible. Her office was at the far end of a corridor in a remote part of the building where she worked, a place where no one ever passed. Day after day she ate her brown-bag lunch in the privacy of her office, rather than mingling with people in the cafeteria. The crowning technique of her isolation was an unlisted telephone number! Yet she could not perceive that she had engineered her loneliness.

This wonderful young woman was convinced that no one could be attracted to her. She feared that if she allowed herself to be visible and found that no one had any interest in her, this revelation would be devastating. To avoid confirmation of her worst fears, she simply made it impossible to be either actively or passively rejected.

The tragedy, of course, is that if she had not withdrawn from people, she would have found that she was desirable, and could have enjoyed the friendship that she craved.

Sometimes you may so adore another person that you cannot conceive why he or she would not give you the time of day. But even wonderful people are only people. Realizing that they are human rather than divine should make it easier to approach them.

44

Just daydreaming about such encounters will get you nowhere.

Make the approach yourself. Don't engage intermediaries.

Don't Precipitate Rejection

*H*uman beings are gregarious creatures. We really do not like to be alone.

What about all those people who are loners? They will readily tell you that they prefer solitude to company.

Many loners are people who crave companionship, but feel they are unlikable. They feel that if they were to seek company, they would be rejected. They therefore avoid relationships. If they do enter into a relationship, they are so certain they will be rejected that they create a situation to precipitate rejection. The torment of anticipating rejection can be worse than the rejection itself.

Not everyone is going to like you, but unless you consider yourself utterly unlikable, about fifty percent of people should like you. In a world with a population of three billion, that gives you one and one-half billion potential friends, and that's quite adequate.

But if you think badly about yourself, then you may become convinced that not even one out of the three billion will like you. If some people do seem to like you, you convince yourself that their feeling is certain to change as soon as they discover "the truth" about you. So why live with the terrible suspense of wondering when the rejection is going to happen? It's so much easier to provoke people and get it over with quickly.

Do you provoke such situations? Why don't you consider the possibility that you really are a likable person?

Just Be Yourself

Some people try to impress everyone with their importance. They may keep aloof and expect others to think that just being in their presence is a distinct privilege, and that being acknowledged by them is an honor of the greatest magnitude. These people are generally seen to be "stuffed shirts," and their companionship is rarely sought.

There are others who wish to impress you with their friendliness. In a way, they are telling you how fortunate you are that they think you to be worthy of their friendship. Their attitude of condescension penetrates the facade of friendliness, and these people, too, are usually avoided.

Just be yourself; people are much more apt to like you for who you really are than for who you pretend to be.

Why Anticipate Having Problems

*P*eople who develop an intimate relationship that is based on true affection are sometimes frightened by the thought that incompatibilities may eventually develop. This may lead them to terminate the relationship. If they follow this pattern, they may deprive themselves of happiness and end up isolated and lonely.

In every close relationship there can be problems, but a little sincere and mutual consideration can usually overcome these.

Don't plan on having problems. If you do, you have two strikes against you before you start.

While it is naive to believe that a relationship will be devoid of any difficulties, there is adequate time to deal with these if and when they arise. If you plan on having problems, you are apt to actually create them.

Accept What Cannot Be Changed

I have seen relationships that have clearly reached the point of being irremediable. Quite often, one partner refuses to accept the inevitable. A jilted lover or spouse may persist in pursuing the other partner, often continuing to protest love and devotion.

In every such case, it appears that true love and devotion are not what is motivating the refusal to give up the relationship. It is rather the inability to accept that one has been rejected. People who have low self-esteem are particularly unable to accept the reality of a rejection, and may take very drastic measures to preserve the relationship.

Countless relationships come to unhappy endings, but after a period of grief, life goes on and new relationships develop.

Hanging on to a relationship that is obviously over is futile, wasteful and painful. It delays the grieving process and the possibility of getting on with life. No one denies that there is great pain in being rejected. But if you accept the inevitable, that pain will eventually disappear and enjoyable new relationships can develop.

Stick With The Winners

*P*eople who have feelings of inadequacy may try to build their self-esteem by choosing as friends people who are obviously inferior to them. Associating with people they think are superior to them is very threatening, and even associating with equals is not too comfortable.

By allying themselves with losers, they can perceive themselves to be winners.

Understanding this adjustment is important because it is often based on an erroneous self-assessment. What is even more important is that there is no stimulation for growth or improvement when one associates with inferiors. It is a known phenomenon in sports that if you play with an opponent that is better than you, your game will improve.

If you find yourself gravitating toward relationships which clearly bring you into contact with persons inferior to yourself, stand back and reconsider. You may feel rather comfortable and secure in the knowledge that you will not be challenged, but if you cannot stand the discomfort of "growing pains," you are not likely to grow.

People are apt to conform to the level of the people with whom they associate. Look about you. If you don't want to resemble your associates, why don't you associate with people you do wish to resemble?

5. EMOTIONS

Know Your Feelings

*I*f someone steps heavily on your toes while passing your seat in a theater, you have several options. You can say, "Please watch where you are going," or "What's the matter with you, you jerk?" Or you can give the person a brisk shove accompanied by an expletive. You can choose how to respond, but not whether you will feel the pain in your foot.

Feelings are not under voluntary control. However, if you know what it is you are feeling, you have options on your response.

If, for whatever reason, you are unaware of what you are feeling, or, as psychologists would say, the feelings are in your unconscious, then you have no control of them and they can then have various harmful affects on you.

Is it okay to be jealous?

Well, let's put it this way. We should not react with hostility because of jealousy, and we should not harbor jealousy. There are ways of reasoning our way out of jealousy.

But in order to extricate yourself from jealousy, you have to first be aware that you are jealous. If you deny that you are jealous, then you are helpless to deal with the feeling.

Don't deny your true feelings and emotions. Rather, learn to control them.

What About Pent-up Emotions?

*F*reud made many important psychological observations. One of these was that when a feeling is repressed, by which is meant that it is so unacceptable that it is driven out of the conscious mind and buried somewhere deep, it may continue to exert its effects on emotions and behavior.

The solution to this is that we should try to become aware of whatever feelings we have so that we can manage them appropriately, something we cannot do if they are buried beyond our awareness.

This is totally different than saying that a person should give free and uncontrolled expression to all his feelings.

You don't have to be restricted by your repressed feelings. The goal is to know what you feel, and to be master of yourself instead of a slave to your impulses.

Be Honest With Yourself

Deceiving other people might not be ethical but you can get away with it. You *can* fool some of the people all of the time.

But if you succeed in deceiving yourself, what have you accomplished? You are then the victim of your own designs.

We are resourceful enough to deal with losses or rejection, but we can't do much in this respect if we don't admit to our hurt feelings.

If your feelings are hurt, don't convince yourself that you are callous and don't care. You might act callous long enough to develop not only a hard exterior but to stifle many of your emotions altogether, and that will not make you a more interesting person.

Don't fool yourself. You can cope with your emotions, but only if you acknowledge them.

A "Quick Fix" Is Not The Answer

Suppose you've consulted a physician because of pain. The physician is able to diagnose the source of the pain and institutes appropriate treatment to cure the problem. It may be appropriate to give you a painkiller for relief while the cause of the pain is being eradicated by the treatment.

But if the doctor cannot find a reason for the pain and therefore cannot remove its cause, prescribing pills and painkillers can be dangerous. If the pain persists, you may become addicted and then have *two* problems: serious drug addiction plus a pain that will not go away because the body has become immune to drugs.

The attitude of, "Let's just feel good now and not worry about the future," is a foolish one.

A cookie, a pill, liquor are all the same. People are only too happy to get relief from their current misery, and whether it's physical or emotional pain, many people will take their relief for the present without consideration for the future.

The people who *should* know better should know better, and should not yield to requests for temporary relief when this can lead to permanent misery.

There's Nothing Wrong With A Good Cry

*F*ar too many people are taking tranquilizing medication. Too often people who are not really emotionally sick use these drugs to escape from real-life problems. At other times people are given medication because others around them cannot tolerate seeing them emotionally distraught.

When tragedy strikes, friends and relatives may push tranquilizers and sedatives onto the bereaved person, and far too often doctors comply by prescribing them.

Grieving may be painful, but it is a healthy outlet when it is justified.

Tranquilizers are medication that should be reserved for sick people. Not all crying is brought on by depression. It may be a healthy emotional outlet which should not be stifled.

If you see someone you know who is grieving, offer to make yourself available. Sometimes bereaved people want to talk about their loss and cry. Sometimes they just need someone to hold their hand, to assure them that they are not alone.

If you want to give something to help a person in grief, don't give something from the drug store. Give of yourself, your company, and your willingness to listen.

6. WORRY

Make Your Worrying Count

*T*hink back. Do you remember worrying about something and subsequently finding out that your worry was unwarranted, and that what you feared might happen never transpired at all?

If worrying were harmless, it would not be much of a problem. But worrying does take its toll. And if you stress your system with excessive worry, it is likely to wear out earlier.

Think positively, and save your worries for when they can accomplish something.

Save Your Energy For The Times When It Makes A Difference

There are may suspenseful circumstances in life, and suspense does produce a great deal of tension. If whatever is going to happen is out of your hands, then it is best to plan to adapt to whatever is going to materialize. Working oneself into a frenzy may result in ulcers but will not in any way affect what is going to happen.

There are enough opportunities in life to plan constructively. Worrying about an eventuality that you can do nothing about is a destructive and foolish expenditure of precious energy.

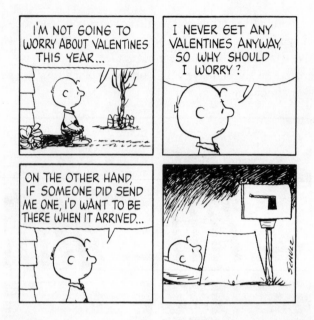

Whether or not you receive a valentine, get an increase in your paycheck, or get a good grade on an exam that you have already taken . . . all these are out of your hands. That is, you do have the opportunity to earn these, but if you have already done whatever you could, further worry about how things are going to turn out is of no use.

If you really want the reward, the time to worry is when you can do something about it. After the event, worry can bring only grief.

If you did not get what you wanted this time, cheer up. You still have another chance.

It's Okay To Keep Your Guard Up

With all the emphasis on avoiding needless worry, we should not lose sight of the fact that there is such a thing as constructive worry.

Reality has an abundance of problems. Some businesses do go bankrupt, some foods may contain harmful additives, and there *are* some drunk drivers on the road.

Worry is not an "all-or-nothing" phenomenon.

"Reasonable." Why is the concept so difficult to define?

Worrywarts think they are being reasonable. Reckless people also think they are being reasonable.

Yet, there is hope that reason can prevail if you try and use it. You don't have to stay awake all night worrying about whether General Motors will collapse, or whether the hot dog you ate will give you cancer, or whether you will be hit by a car on the way to work in the morning.

Just be careful and use common sense.

7. GUILT

Don't Let Guilt Push You Around

Nothing motivates like guilt. The thought that if we fail to do something, we will be tormented by our conscience, is a difficult one to dismiss.

Some people are masters at manipulating through guilt. Parents are, by far, the most adroit at this skill.

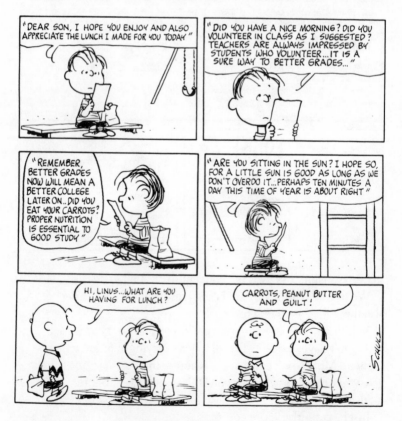

Succumbing to guilt is like paying blackmail. There is no end to the demands that can be made on you. Guilt can override even the most important commitments you have made or other responsibilities that you have assumed.

It is unwise to be dominated by guilt, and it is certainly unwise as well as cruel to manipulate others by guilt.

You might succeed in getting something done for you by invoking guilt. But it will be done with much resentment and cost you the affection the other person had for you.

There are valid reasons why you should do things for others. Guilt is not one of them. So, when it comes to guilt as motivation, "Neither a giver nor a taker be." Either way you are the loser.

You Can Be Sorry, But Don't Be Too Sorry

Regretting something for which we were remiss is a commendable trait. But this commendable trait can backfire if carried to extremes. Sometimes the guilt can be so severe that we become paralyzed and think, "What's the use? I can't do anything right anyway."

Instead of going ahead with correcting our mistakes, we then do nothing.

If you've done something wrong, do feel sorry. Go ahead and apologize, and, if any kind of restitution is required, go ahead and make it.

See what you can do to avoid repetition of the mistake, and then go on with living. In fact, since most of us learn only from mistakes, chalk this up as a valuable learning experience.

If you allow your guilt to weigh you down, you'll get nowhere fast.

Learn From The Past, Then Forget It

Someone said that the only thing we learned from history is that humans seemed to have never learned from history.

Making mistakes is unfortunate, but seems to be an unavoidable fact of life. Making the same mistake twice, however, is avoidable. And if someone has already made the mistake for you, you are lucky! You can learn from other people's mistakes.

But except for learning from mistakes of the past, there is really no purpose in dwelling on them.

One of the reasons people ruminate about the past is that it keeps them from having to deal with the present. To some people, dealing with the present can be so difficult that they will do anything to avoid it.

So what are the alternatives? If you daydream about the future, you may be accused of being shiftless, lazy, or good for nothing. But if you dwell on mistakes of the past, that seems to be more ac-

ceptable. In fact, you might even find some willing listeners. Some
people who have nothing to do just love to listen to other people's
woes.

But ruminating about the past will get you nowhere. So go
ahead and learn from the past whatever you can, and then put it behind you. Remember, there is nothing you can do to change it,
but you can use its lessons to improve your future.

You Don't Have To Be A Martyr

Martyrdom is not an infrequent psychological finding. People
who feel they have been deprived of something wallow in misery
and self-pity instead of seeing what it is they did or failed to do that
resulted in the deprivation. This, of course, gets them nowhere because they do not take the necessary steps to get whatever it is they
want. They are too occupied with feeling sorry for themselves.

In some dysfunctional families, as in the family of an alcoholic,
martyrdom is common. One or more of the family members feels
sorry for himself or herself, and the gratification of being a martyr

allows them to continue absorbing the abusive behavior or suffering continuing deprivation.

Don't be a martyr. You don't have to suffer.

You Are Not Responsible For Everything

What is it within us that makes us crave guilt?

A crazed, brutal murderer scribbles on the wall of his victim's home, "Please stop me!", and society assumes responsibility for his crimes.

Criminals kill, maim, and plunder, and yet we may feel sorry for these victims of an unjust society. If only we had given them a better chance at life, they would have been paragons of virtue.

People must be responsible for their own behavior.

Many things enter into the formation of a person's character.

People are all born into varying circumstances, but how people use the ingredients of their particular lives is up to them.

You are responsible for what *you* do. You do not have to assume the guilt for anyone else's behavior.

Magical Thinking

Some people are tormented by guilt feelings because they believe that they caused harm to someone by wishing him evil.

This belief probably has its origin early in infancy. The infant
who is hungry and wishes to be fed is often fed even before he cries.
This may lead to development of the idea that he controls his
mother with his wishes. It's a small jump from, "When I wish my
mother to feed me, she does," to, "When I wish for things, they
happen."

In some people, this idea persists into adult life, and can result
in guilt feelings.

Logic to the contrary may not be enough. However, we should
learn from experience that our wishes do not make things happen.
If they did, more than half the world would probably be dead.

When guilt is the result of improper behavior, we should make amends to whomever we've offended and resolve not to repeat such behavior. But guilt that is felt for no valid reason, such as for having bad thoughts, can be very tenacious and can interfere with our daily lives.

Don't let unwarranted feelings of guilt become a burden.

Guilt Icing

Why people do it is inexplicable.

You have earned something or someone gives you a treat: a tasty meal, a vacation, a new house or whatever.

Just when you are ready to enjoy it, someone reminds you how fortunate you are in contrast to the people in Ethiopia who are dying of hunger, or the poor in Appalachia who live in squalor, or the refugees in Pakistan who don't have a roof over their heads to shield them from the torrential monsoon rains.

Whatever pleasure you may have enjoyed has been taken away.

Needless to say, you should not inflict guilt feelings on others and destroy their enjoyment.

But what can you do to prevent others from inflicting them on you?

My little girl set me straight on this question. We once told her that she had to finish everything on her plate because, "Those poor children in Africa have nothing to eat."

She just looked up and said, "And if I finish everything on my plate, then the children in Africa won't be hungry anymore?"

Such a small amount of logic can set things straight. If you can contribute to help unfortunate people, by all means do so. But your being miserable will not make other people one bit happier.

Go ahead and enjoy what you have.

You Deserve To Be Happy

*I*t almost sounds silly to assert that some people are afraid to be happy, yet it's true.

Some people are afraid to enjoy something because they think they will be hurt if they lose it. Others may go even further and think that they don't deserve to be happy, and that any happiness they have will therefore be taken from them. Some people believe that there is virtue only in suffering, and that happiness is the work of the devil.

Sure there are side effects to happiness, but they are generally only the ones you manufacture yourself.

People should enjoy things on a human level, with respect and consideration for others, and avoid harmful excesses. To deny oneself healthy enjoyment seems rather foolish.

If you are plagued by feelings of guilt that make you consider yourself undeserving of happiness, take the appropriate steps to eliminate this guilt. See your spiritual advisor or psychotherapist, or both if necessary. But don't run away from happiness.

8. DEPRESSION

Depression Can Be a Family Disease

When I was in psychiatric training, a hospitalized depressed patient was given a weekend home visit. On her return she stated that the weekend was very enjoyable and that she was very pleased with it.

I was therefore surprised when her husband called to report that the weekend had been absolutely terrible. His wife was irritable, had moped, and made life miserable for everyone else.

I consulted my supervisor about this discrepancy, and he said that he did not see any discrepancy whatever. Both accounts were accurate. She indeed made everyone miserable, and apparently thoroughly enjoyed it.

Some types of depression are due to chemical imbalances of the system. These people suffer intense emotional pain. They generally do not have any intention of hurting anyone.

But there are other types of depression, probably not of physical origin, where it is quite evident that the person is trying to avenge himself at the expense of others. People with this type of depression may be provocatively irritable and seem to derive a weird sort of comfort from their depression. In such cases, the worst one can do is to allow this mechanism to work.

People with a chemical imbalance type of depression will do anything to feel better. Because they feel depleted and hopeless, they may not be easily motivated to do things, but they will try anything that offers hope of relief. People whose depression is their way of acting out, make it quite clear that they don't want to feel undepressed.

In fact, this type of depression seems to give the person a weird kind of comfort.

If you're angry at someone, don't act out your anger through depression. If someone around you is depressed, be guided by their doctor's advice. Sometimes your consideration and help is essential, and sometimes you just cannot cater to their behavior. It is important to have competent guidance on which is which.

Get On With Life

Depression is such an uncomfortable feeling that it seems inconceivable that anyone would want to hold onto it. Yet this does happen.

Have you ever felt you can't go on with life because you are unable to get over some painful experience?

Most people survive disappointments and tragic happenings, and go on with life, unless they are so afraid to take the normal risks of everyday living that they exploit their depression as an excuse for not progressing.

Don't let unpleasant experiences become your excuse for opting out of life.

9. RESPONSIBLITY

Don't Blame Others For Your Failures

Accepting responsibility for failure is always difficult, so we look for a way out or a way to transfer the blame.

When there is a need to blame someone, all rules of logic are apt to be suspended. We may place the blame on someone who was not involved in the project to the slightest degree.

There is only one thing that is not quite accurate in the strip above. Peppermint Patty recognizes the fact that she is unjustly placing the blame on someone else. In real life such insight rarely occurs.

Of course, if it were all "Chuck's" fault, then there is nothing Peppermint Patty must do to get better grades. If it is her own fault, then she must make a greater effort. She must study, do her homework, pay attention in class. Obviously it is much easier to think of her failure as someone else's fault.

Don't look for someone to blame when something goes wrong. Look instead for ways to correct matters.

Any Excuse Will Do

When you don't want to accept responsibility for your failure, any excuse will do. The excuse doesn't have to be logical. In fact, it may be patently absurd, but if you need it, it will do.

Some people could win contests by completing the sentence, "I failed because . . ." in twenty-five words or less. They could submit multiple entries, none of which would say, "because I didn't try hard enough."

Certainly there are circumstances beyond our control that
thwart even the best undertakings. But if you look at your own en-
deavors first with a sincere desire to know the truth, you will often
find lack of effort to be responsible for the failure.

Examine Your Own Efforts First

There are many times when we don't succeed because we are
derelict in our efforts. Lack of interest, distraction or just plain lazi-

ness may result in our not doing the kinds of things that are necessary for a successful result.

On the one hand people who have poor self-esteem are apt to blame themselves for everything. On the other, they may resist blaming themselves for anything. Sometimes seeing a shortcoming in oneself is just too threatening, and it is so much easier to feel that one is an innocent victim of things that are beyond one's control.

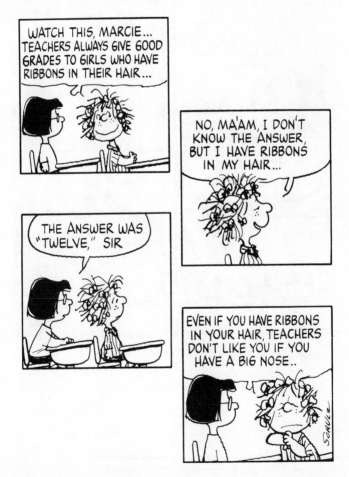

When things turn out unfavorably for you, try to look objectively at what happened. If you find that you made a mistake, don't let this shatter you. We all make mistakes. Recognizing where you went wrong allows you to take corrective measures to avoid making the same mistake next time around.

If you find yourself blaming others or things beyond your control for your lack of success, stop. It's possible that the responsibility is shared but the best place to begin looking for what went wrong is in what you know you did or did not do.

Scapegoating may give you a temporary sense of relief, but won't do anything for your ultimate success.

10. COPING

So You Had A Bad Experience

"*I*nto every life a little rain must fall." Okay, but rain is rain, and does not have to be a thunderstorm or a tornado.

Even when unpleasant things happen, we can often magnify or minimize their impact, depending on how we interpret them. We do have some leeway in interpretation of such matters.

Imagine, for whatever reason, you are a wallflower at a party. Sometimes people do things to alienate others. Sometimes people withdraw from others because of the conviction that others will reject them. They don't even give people a chance to like them!

If you see yourself as being basically a good person, yet find yourself less popular than you would like to be, investigate what it is that is interfering with your popularity. If, instead, you convince yourself that you are fundamentally no good and that this is an unalterable fact, you are apt to do nothing to change things.

Give yourself a break. You may be a much better person than you think you are. Most people are.

Take Disappointments In Stride

Allowing suspense to build up to destructive tension is bad enough, but if the suspense is terminated by a disappointing result, it is important to sit back and make the best possible adjustment.

Some people may be so devastated by a disappointment that they cannot accept it as reality. They may then try to deny the obvious or to change the unchangeable. At best, such efforts are futile. At worst, they cause even more misery than the disappointment itself.

If you have received a low grade on the exam, don't confront the professor with obscenities. If you did not receive the pay raise you expected, don't impulsively curse the boss and quit the job. Take some time to cool off and think. If you come to the conclusion that you have been dealt with unfairly, try to talk reasonably with your instructor or employer. Sometimes this does work.

Dispassionate analysis of what has happened may suggest some constructive actions to improve the situation—a bit more study, a better work attitude, or, in the event of a social disappointment, examining your ways of relating to people. Bounce your ideas off a friend.

This way, you should be able to avoid further disappointments.

Bad Things Do Happen To Good People

*E*ver since human beings began to think, they have sought to solve the mystery of why there is suffering in the world. All the great theologians and philosophers have tackled this problem. But if you are honest in assessing all their theories, you will conclude that there is just no satisfactory, logical answer.

Some people say that all suffering is divine retribution. I wonder who gave them direct access to the mind of God?

As a matter of faith, I can believe that God rewards good and punishes evil. But when it comes to individual examples, I cannot claim to know why anything specific happened to anyone, and I don't believe that other people can either.

There is nothing more cruel than to add insult to injury, and tell people who are suffering that they are being punished for something they did. If you can't help or comfort people who are suffering, don't make their pain worse by blaming them for it.

Anticipate Fun Rather Than Misery

*P*eople are prone to various moods, many of which occur for no apparent reason. We are capable of feeling lousy without any discernible cause.

Bad moods are likely to fade away. That is, if you let them. But if you hang on to them or, worse yet, take them as omens, you not only prolong them, but actually create a situation where things go wrong so that you will have adequate cause to be in a bad mood.

If you wake up in the morning with the feeling that something terrible is going to happen, don't take it seriously. You might have had a frightening dream that, although you cannot remember, is still causing after-effects. Or you may have had one of those changes in body hormones that scientists have discovered can alter your mood.

Go call up a friend who doesn't mind being called early in the morning. Have a book of funny stories available and read a few. If you are religious, say a few prayers, especially the kind that stimulate joy.

The least constructive thing you can do is to believe that you are destined to do something stupid.

A Positive Attitude Is A Great Pain-killer

We all know that how we feel emotionally can affect how we feel physically.

If this is the day you are due to pick up a handsome bonus, the arthritic hip pain or the headache you feel are negligible. If this is the day for your IRS audit, the same discomfort can make you sick enough to warrant emergency hospitalization.

Of course, major illnesses can disable anyone. But discomforts that are not life threatening do not have to be disabling, unless you allow them to be.

If you believe you're likely to lose the game, that the first pitch will probably be hit out of the ballpark, every muscle in your body is apt to hurt.

If you've really been a consistent loser, why don't you go for some professional counseling or therapy? Maybe you shouldn't be playing baseball, maybe you're in the wrong job, or maybe you're allowing a difficult family situation to disturb your function. Whatever, get some help.

But if you function the way most of us do—win some, lose some—then think more positively. And don't let minor aches and pains dictate your life.

Results Often Follow Expectations

While there are many situations that are beyond our control, there are still countless others that we can control. A successful adjustment to life requires being able to distinguish which things are beyond our control and which are not.

A defeatist attitude can bring about defeat, and we can encourage a self-perpetuating, vicious cycle by expecting to lose, which often causes us to lose, which then proves to us that our expectations were indeed right. So if we label ourselves as losers, we are likely to become losers.

The sun getting in your eyes and making you miss the ball may be unavoidable, but allowing your vision of the future to blind you is certainly avoidable.

Sometimes we may not like to think that it was our attitude that led to failure, and so we blame it on things beyond our control: the weather, the economy, and especially other people.

Virgil said, "Birds fly because they think they can."

Attitudes can be controlled more easily than you think. Think success and you are more likely to succeed.

11. TAKING POSITIVE ACTION

Get Things Done Now

*P*utting things off is so common that it can hardly be considered abnormal behavior. Maybe there is nothing really wrong with putting things off once in a while. If we miss an important opportunity, we will learn from the experience and be a bit more diligent next time.

But there are some people for whom procrastination seems to be a way of life. They never get things done on time, and even when they lose out because of this, they don't change their ways. They appear to be unable to learn from experience. They adhere to procrastination as though they were dedicated to it as a philosophy of life.

You've probably heard someone say "Don't put things off" a thousand times since you were a child. So there is not much purpose in saying it again.

But you might just examine your habits to see if your way of putting things off is similar to that of other people.

Are you habitually late? Do you ask for an extension on your income tax return every year? How often do you pay penalties for not remitting payments on time? Add up what your procrastination has cost you. How much have you wasted in money, in time and in missed opportunities?

. . . But Don't Go To The Other Extreme

*J*ust as excessive procrastination is a bad trait, so is undue anxiety about getting things done immediately as though there were no tomorrow.

People who feel themselves to be constantly under pressure of time are referred to as "Type-A Personalities." This behavior takes its toll by causing high blood pressure, migraine headaches and heart attacks. Don't misunderstand the saying "live today as though it were your last" to mean that you have to do everything today that you planned to do over the next year or two.

Neither procrastination nor panic of delay are healthy. A reasonable middle ground is possible.

The fact is that most of us that are here today will still be here tomorrow.

If you receive your income tax form on January 20, it does not have to be completed on that very same day, but neither do you have to wait in line at the post office on April 15. How about doing it some time in February or early March? And, if this were your last day, you still don't have to panic. Just behave toward others in such a way that if you will not have the opportunity to make amends, you will not have left behind any unfinished business.

Decisions, Decisions

S ome people agonize over decisions, even to the point of being paralyzed by the inability to make decisions, and they end up doing nothing at all.

Important decisions should, of course, not be made upon whim and without adequate consideration of the pros and cons on each side. But when the issue at hand is one which is of relatively little importance, why agonize over it?

It seems that to some people, things which should be trivial are given undue importance.

If there were any way in which one of the two choices was really superior to the other, there wouldn't be any doubt about which one one to choose. So if the choices are really that close, and the issue is not one of major importance, why be indecisive? You really can't go seriously wrong either way.

I've seen some people simply unable to decide which color car they want or what color carpet to choose. If you don't have a clear preference, then both options are so close that it shouldn't make too much of a difference.

Not Choosing Is Still A Choice

*P*eople who lack confidence in their own judgment are apt to take the easiest way, essentially allowing others to make decisions for them.

This is not too serious a problem if it involves styles of clothing or home furnishings. But when moral or ethical issues are involved, it is a mistake to abdicate one's responsibility to choose for oneself.

One cannot avoid making a choice. The decision to conform is really choosing not to choose for oneself, and that, too, is a moral choice.

In matters requiring special knowledge, it is, of course, wise to accept the opinion of experts.

When moral decisions are to be made, we should listen carefully to those who can speak authoritatively on the issues, but the ultimate decision should be a personal one.

Sometimes one can find an individual of such stature that one is willing to accept his or her word as final on moral issues. This is fine, if one is consistent and does not just subscribe to those decisions that one finds agreeable.

But unless you have a trusted mentor, don't be wishy-washy. Assert your right and responsibility to choose.

What's The Problem?

It is common practice that when an athletic team is performing poorly, the manager is dismissed. (I have often wondered why it is that the next team that hires this seemingly incompetent manager so often goes on to succeed.)

It is human nature to want change for the sake of change.

Buying a new garment can often get one out of a depressed mood, and moving to another city and starting over again may get one out of a rut.

There is a catch to this behavior. Sometimes people try to manipulate circumstances to improve their lives when what they should really be manipulating is themselves. It is tragic to see people blame their spouses for their misery and terminate relationships that could really be workable. It is particularly pathetic when one tries manipulation after manipulation until the final discovery that the problem is really within oneself. Sometimes this awareness comes at a much later stage in life when the opportunities for growth and productivity are greatly diminished.

Maybe you do need some kind of a change. But if the change you're contemplating significantly affects the lives of other people, such as your spouse or children, you should certainly consult an expert before jumping to the conclusion that you have found the real source of your problem.

Be Careful About What You Think You Need

One day I received a call for help from a man who was using a number of street drugs, including heroin and alcohol. We discussed what would be involved in treatment for his problem, and I suggested a medication that would help him avoid alcohol. He said he was reluctant to take this medication because "I don't want to put anything into my body that isn't absolutely essential."

One can only conclude that when this man used the various toxic chemicals, his craving for them was so intense that for him they were "absolutely essential."

Whether it's a matter of things we would like to eat or drink or things we would like to own, we should be aware that our desire for something can be so strong that it ceases to become a luxury or option, and becomes an "absolute essential."

Get Your Priorities In Order

Some decisions in life are of major importance, some are of lesser importance, and some involve such trivia as to be virtually insignificant. It would appear reasonable that we should direct most of our attention to major items and less attention to the lesser ones.

Sometimes our sense of priorities may be distorted by psychological factors. For example, a young woman whose self-esteem is low may so invest in her external appearance that a tiny skin blemish may give her greater concern than her career. A student who has written himself off as an academic failure may devote more time to his clothes than to his studies.

What may appear as trivial to some people may be as important as career decisions to others.

I've seen some people show more concern and do more research on what car to buy than on what school their child should attend. We probably all know people who are more meticulous about the floral arrangements at the wedding than the person their child is marrying.

Rank the various aspects of your life according to their importance. Then calculate how much time you spend on each.

Look For Effective Solutions

You might get rich by winning the lottery, or the boss just might have the whim to promote people whose names begin with "Z". But don't count on it.

Some people do not achieve the goals they seek because of lack of effort. It may be just plain laziness. Sometimes they do ask for advice and guidance, but if whatever they are told to do does not fit into their comfortable way of life, they may not make the necessary changes. Rather, they may turn to others for advice until they hear a solution that pleases them.

If the advice you get for solving a problem doesn't suit you, don't reject it out of hand. If you keep on looking until someone gives you a solution that you like, take a real good look. It's probably what you've been doing all along.

Many good things in life don't come without a struggle.

Evolution, Not Revolution

There is much to be said for change. Human beings are far from perfect, individually and collectively. But for change to be constructive, it should occur at a pace at which it can be absorbed and integrated as well as evaluated.

As unpleasant as it is to be in total darkness, sudden exposure to a very bright light can be painful and even harmful. Also, although obesity is certainly unhealthy, doctors warn against a too rapid reduction in weight. The body needs time to adjust.

In an age of high-speed technology, it is so easy to lose tolerance. We come to believe that there must be a microwave for everything.

Growth and development in children is delightful to behold. But what seems so rapid is not all that sudden. Babies crawl before they walk, and they do fall many times before they master the art of ambulation. And children don't begin talking by reciting the "Gettysburg Address." Furthermore, in all their new experiences,

they are guided by the love and care of those who have already experienced this behavior.

Of course you should use your energies to bring about change.
But make sure it is constructive change. Learning to talk without
the benefit of people who have mastered speech will result in
meaningless babbling.

Enthusiasm: Less Is More

*T*oday is the day you will finally clean out the garage. All of it. It
will be as spic-and-span as a hospital corridor.

The telethon on the terrible disease was so moving that you will
not rest until you have knocked on every door in the neighborhood
to raise money for the research necessary to find a cure.

The pastor's sermon was really inspiring. It's time to think of
the important things in life instead of indulging in all those silly
pastimes.

What enthusiasm and dedication! Does anyone have a
stopwatch?

The problem is that when we bite off more than we can chew, we tend to spit it out. If your goals are too ambitious, the "all-or-nothing" law goes into effect, and the "nothing" usually wins.

Begin by removing just some of the junk from the garage. Resolve to make three or four calls for the charity drive. Try to do one of the things the pastor suggested. Bite off only what you can comfortably chew and swallow.

Ask For Help When You Need It

*B*eing independent and self-sufficient is, indeed, very commendable. Like any other good trait when taken to the extreme, it can backfire.

Some people seem to have so much pride that they refuse to ask for help even when their need is genuine. Perhaps it is because deep in their heads they feel themselves to be inadequate, and they believe that asking for help confirms their worst fear about themselves. They interpret accepting help as proof of their inadequacy.

The problem is that when we refuse to accept the help that we really need and insist on doing everything for ourselves, we may end up with some costly mistakes that could have been avoided.

Heads may be wiser, but they may occasionally need the support of arms. It is senseless to let the head suffer just because you might not want to reveal your necessity to lean on the arms. Don't be afraid to impose upon others for genuinely needed help. Most people are happy to oblige because they enjoy feeling useful. Obviously, arms can get tired if they are leaned on too often or too heavily, so don't overdo it.

Don't you like to be of help to others when you can? Well, if you can't accept help, what right do you have to give it?

Don't Quit Before You Start

One child can be given a room full of toys and see the electric train as a potential source of being electrocuted, the hammer and nails set as producing punctures resulting in lockjaw, the bike as something from which to fall and sustain a skull fracture. Another will look at a pile of manure and gleefully conclude there must be a pony around somewhere.

Attitudes are everything. Major calamities such as earthquakes, fires and terrible diseases do occur. But if all you see is calamity, it is most likely inside yourself rather than out in the world.

Life abounds with opportunities. If you try, you may succeed.

It is rather unlikely that you will succeed all the time, but if you do things reasonably well, you can enjoy your successes and write off the failures as the natural cost of doing business.

Some people are so devastated by the thought of possible failure that they are too frightened to try anything. But if you do nothing, then you are a real loser.

There is no logical reason why failure by inaction should be considered any better than failure by action.

Take that first step.

You Can Enjoy Success

Some people start ventures, and just when they seem to be on the verge of success, they do something to undermine them. When this is more than an isolated occurrence, but seems to be a pattern, there must be a reason for it.

You've heard it said that some people are afraid of success. But that sounds so strange. Why would anyone fear success?

Success almost always means new responsibilities, and some people like to avoid these. Succeeding at something also means that you can no longer hide under the guise of being a congenital failure.

For people who have repeatedly failed, failure has its comforts. They are familiar with it. It is a known territory.

Success may appear attractive, but if it's something new to you, it is unknown territory, and the unknown can be very frightening.

When you were an infant, you crawled on all fours. Since you no longer do so, you obviously mastered the art of walking, although you undoubtedly fell a few times before getting the knack of it.

So you've already had the experience of persevering at something in spite of failure, and trading in the old method for a more efficient one.

Capitalize on that experience. Don't be afraid of success.

12. VALUES

Meaning Of Life

Philosophers and theologians have written copiously on the meaning of life. Rationalists have sought to arrive at the meaning of life based on pure reason and without recourse to a supernatural power. Transcendentalists have found meaning only by invoking a Being external to the world as we know it.

To many people, the meaning of life is none of these. They operate on a plane where deprivation of one's needs and wants makes life meaningless, and satisfaction of one's desires is all the meaning they seek.

Every person is, of course, free to ascribe to any concept whatever meaning he wishes. It would be well, though, to not deceive yourself. If what you really want is to be physically content, don't pretend to be concerned about more lofty ideas.

Some people's concepts of meaning and purpose do not extend beyond their stomachs.

Know What You Stand For

Some people seem to be charter members of the loyal opposition. What they oppose is really secondary, as long as they can oppose something. They quickly unfurl their banner and become militant about something, but as soon as their cause fades they quickly find a new cause to champion.

These people should not be confused with those who are really thoughtful protagonists or antagonists. These latter people may have some worthwhile ideas that are worthy of consideration.

How can you tell a thoughtful and sincere advocate of a cause from someone who is just looking for something to do?

Most sincere advocates have positions that they can defend. They don't make a lot of noise. When you have good reason and evidence to support your position, you don't have to yell. Thoughtful people will also generally adhere to the issues at hand. Windbags will pick a fight for silly reasons.

By all means, listen to thoughtful people. But don't pay any attention to windbags.

Real Values Shouldn't Change

The old double standard has been around since time immemorial. The most ancient codes of ethics warn against conflict of interest, because when our personal interest is at stake, our judgment can undergo drastic transformation.

Looking out for one's own interest is not at all reprehensible. What is not acceptable is to advocate something as being true and good when it is really self-serving and may not be true and good at all.

Unfortunately, personal gain not only affects our judgment, but can do so in a way that makes us unable to recognize that we are acting in self-interest rather than in the interest of truth and justice.

Try to be alert to having your judgments influenced by personal interests. Try and place yourself in other people's positions, and see how you would react if you were them. Sometimes this helps.

There is part of you that is likely to hold on to the real truth, and will not accept a compromise. If you are swayed by personal interests to alter your convictions, you may gain in the short term, but the agony of a guilty conscience in the long term is not worth it.

Speak Out

The secret ballot is an important method to eliminate favoritism or fear of retaliation as factors that could interfere with the democratic process.

But that is where secrecy should stop.

When people wish to voice their opinions, secrecy is out of place.

If you don't have the fortitude to stand up for your conviction, it isn't much of a conviction.

Whether in government or in the citizenry, we should not be ambivalent. Make a reasoned judgment and have sufficient faith in your opinion to defend it.

Don't Be Obstinate, But Do Respect Your Judgment

*P*art of the pattern of people who have low self-esteem is to readily yield to others' opinions. Although they may be initially convinced of the validity of their thinking, their lack of self-confidence makes them retreat from the slightest challenge. Everyone else knows more than they do.

These people lack the strength of their own convictions and are easily swayed to any passing opinion. Even the acceptance of another person's opinion may not be of long duration, since accepting that another person is right is in itself their own judgment, which they consider so unreliable.

If you believe you should not come to conclusions without adequate consideration of all the issues involved, it follows that you should have faith in your own judgments.

If your judgment is challenged, don't be obstinately defiant and refuse to consider another viewpoint. On the other hand, don't yield without appropriate analysis of your position. You have as much right to your opinion as other people have to theirs.

Don't Tailor Justice To Your Own Fancy

*F*or people to live together, there must be reliable standards of right and wrong, and these standards should apply to rich and poor alike. When any society begins to apply one set of rules to some of its citizens and another set to others, its system of justice breaks down.

Idealism is wonderful when it is not self-serving. Some people's idealism, however, doesn't seem to extend beyond their stomach or purse. If either is empty, their beliefs may change radically.

If you pass a playground, you are likely to hear a child cry out, "That's not fair!". You can be sure that the kid has just lost in the game he is playing. Winners don't complain.

But when we become mature adults, our thinking should mature along with our bodies. What is right is right whether it benefits us or not. Wrong is wrong even if it is to our advantage.

Idealism Is Not Always Pure And Simple

There is a story about a wealthy man who had a chauffeur who was an avowed socialist. The man had no objection to the chauffeur's faithful attendance at his regular socialist party meetings, and was therefore surprised one evening to discover that the chauffeur was home instead of attending the party meeting.

When asked why he was not at his meeting, the chauffeur responded, "At the last meeting we were told that after the revolution, all wealth will be divided equally, and that every man, woman and child will receive $4,100.00.

"But," the chauffeur continued, "I already have $4,200.00." Some idealism is limited to whom it may benefit.

Some people have ethics to which they will adhere even at great cost to themselves. Others have ethics that recede under pressure.

Ethics are not only a subject for sermons or seminars. Ethics play a major part in one's self-respect.

What kind of ethics do you believe in?

Might Doesn't Make Right

When people want to dominate others or take something from them, they run into problems of conscience. They may be tormented by their own sense of decency or be confronted by those who oppose their actions.

If you cannot resist temptation, that may be bad enough, but at least you may feel the pangs of your conscience and decide that doing something wrong is just not worth it. But if you deceive yourself that what you are doing is really right, then you may never have a chance to correct your behavior.

If you have some desires that would result in your doing wrong, don't delude yourself that wrong is right.

13. DEALING WITH OTHERS

Be Sensitive To Others' Feelings

*T*here are many self-help groups made up of people who have experienced certain problems and are willing to share their hope, strength and courage with others.

One of the gratifying rewards of associating with recovering alcoholics and addicts is that they are people who have suffered, who remember their suffering, and who are generally very empathic with others who suffer.

Many of us ascribe to the victory ethic, and there is nothing wrong with that. Winning is an excellent motivation and most of us exert effort because there is something we wish to achieve.

Not every victory entails a corresponding loss, but as an adversary in games or other competition, one can win only if someone else loses.

Basking in the glow of triumph is a pleasure, but if you are the winner in a competitive situation, just remember, someone has lost and is probably hurting.

It is as important to be a good winner as it is to be a good loser.

The Mighty Tongue

Many people are very critical of the mass media. We hear much about irresponsible journalism, and how unjust it is to pillory someone, particularly when it may not be possible to undo the damage if the accusations turn out to be wrong.

It would be worth knowing if all those who are critical of the media exercise restraint in talking derogatorily about others. A person can be harmed by irresponsible gossip in the neighborhood just as by an article in the newspaper.

You may be right about irresponsible journalism, and your expression of righteous indignation may or may not have an impact on its practice.

But there is one type of character assassination that you can do a great deal about, and that is your own maligning of others.

Journalists who ruin people's characters are motivated by a desire to be considered good reporters. Individuals who malign others are probably trying to make themselves appear better by degrading other people. Both are selfish and inconsiderate.

Don't put down other people to build yourself up.

Don't Knock Others When They're Down

*P*eople make mistakes. Sometimes they do so unintentionally, in which case they should be forgiven. Sometimes they do so out of selfishness, and if their careless or selfish behavior injures others, they indeed need to be reprimanded or punished.

But too often our very sophisticated society smells blood and goes after someone with a vengeance that can be just as reprehensible as the act that is being condemned.

There is a fine line between coddling anti-social or irresponsible behavior on the one hand, and being merciless on the other. Perhaps it is not such a fine line after all, because there seems to be plenty of latitude between the two.

Punishment as retribution can be defended. Punishment as a deterrent also makes sense. But getting gratification out of seeing someone suffer is indefensible and indicates the presence of sick emotions.

Punishment of an offense requires that the offender be "injured." But that should suffice. Adding insult to injury does not degrade others. It only degrades ourselves.

Make Your Communications Sincere

Do you know why some people feel more comfortable relating to animals than to other human beings? Because animals convey what they feel, and their communication can be trusted. If they are angry, they growl, and if they are pleased, they purr or wag their tails or something. But since they can't talk, they have no way of communicating anything other than what they feel.

People are different. We are sophisticated beings with the ability of verbal communication. So we may say one thing and mean another.

What we may not realize is that we also use nonverbal methods of animal communication, but this behavior is not under our voluntary control. We can control what we say, but what we really feel gets communicated some other way. If the two messages are in conflict, the communication is confusing at best.

If you don't think a person has a chance in a million to succeed, tell him so if you're going to tell him anything. If you think that he can succeed this time in spite of past performances, then tell him that.

The best reason not to lie is not because it is unethical or immoral but because most people are not good liars, at least not when it comes to more personal relationships when feelings are at least as important as facts.

So don't think one thing and say another, because your spoken message is apt to be hopelessly confusing. The only certainty that will emerge is that you can't be trusted.

Silence Can Be Golden

There is a time to listen and there is a time to speak. An old Chinese proverb says that God created people with two ears and only one mouth, so that we should listen twice as much as we speak.

Listening is absorbing knowledge, like depositing money in a bank account. Speaking is dispensing what we know, like a bank withdrawal. If withdrawals exceed deposits, checks become worthless.

Since no one can really listen without talking, we may end up with deficits if we talk too much.

If we did a careful analysis of how often we ended up "with a mouthful of water," we would probably discover that many such experiences could have been avoided if we had not talked too much.

Singing can be most pleasant at the right time and place. Wise words, well chosen and spoken at the right time and place, can be very valuable.

Be careful that you don't trip over your tongue.

It Depends On Who Has The Problem

The magnitude of a problem usually depends on how immediately it affects us.

If the wind blows a cinder into your eye, you can be so uncomfortable that you can't do anything until it is removed. The fact that when the cinder appears on the tip of the cotton swab it is so tiny as to be almost imperceptible does not make the discomfort any less. When something affects us in a very sensitive area, a tiny speck can feel like a mountain.

This is readily apparent when we experience something, but we are not too aware of this when others are affected.

How often have you tried to cheer people up by telling them that they are not as bad off as others? What did you feel like when you were on the receiving end of such brilliant consolation?

We should use our own experience to guide us in trying to help others. It is quite normal to feel our own hunger following a skipped lunch much more intensely than the frank starvation of people in a remote area of the world.

Be considerate of other people when their problems appear to be insignificant to you. They may be major problems to them.

Cast Your Bread Upon The Waters

*I*deally, we should do what is right because it is right, and avoid doing wrong because it is wrong.

Whoever wrote in the book of Ecclesiastes about casting your bread upon the waters understood human nature very thoroughly. When the purest of thoughts is not enough of a motivation, at least be practical. A good deed today may someday be repaid, and an unkind act may eventually be avenged.

Elephants aren't the only ones who do not forget. People whose feelings are hurt tend to remember for a long time as well.

Not everyone is ready to forgive other people's thoughtless actions, and we must admit that we ourselves sometimes find it difficult to do.

So to avoid unnecessary grief in the future, live the Golden Rule, if not selflessly, then do so selfishly.

Understanding Should Be Mutual

The world is comprised of a variety of components, some of which seem to be in conflict with one another.

Being different does not necessarily mean being in conflict. Peaceful coexistence can be a very satisfactory arrangement when there is mutual respect for other people's ideas and beliefs.

Trouble arises when people become suspicious of other people's motives, or when they are so insecure about their own values that they fear they will be vulnerable to other ideas. This is when fanaticism is likely to occur.

Humanity has endured so much strife, suffering, and loss of life, that we can easily understand why some people are pacifists.

However, even something as precious as peace may come at an exorbitant cost. Patrick Henry's famous statement, "Give me liberty or give me death," said it well. Sometimes even life itself may be sacrificed in order to protect inalienable human rights.

Certainly we must make an effort to understand others, but this should not be a one-way street. We need to be understood as well as to understand.

Why Not Diversify?

As kids, we were told not to put all our eggs into one basket. As grownups, we are advised to diversify our investments.

Maybe there is something to these suggestions.

Too many unsinkable ships have been sunk. Corporations that were certain to outlive mankind itself have gone bankrupt. Nothing is absolutely safe.

So why not diversify?

Your spouse will be forever loyal to you and as enraptured with you throughout eternity as on your honeymoon. I hope that's true, but don't count on it.

Your children, who have been very loving and devoted, will always be close to you and will always provide you with love and companionship. Again, I hope so, but don't count on that either.

Why not cultivate more friendships? Join organizations that are dedicated to worthwhile causes. Develop interests and skills and outdoor activities, and pick up some sedentary hobbies. Learn how to appreciate various types of art and music. Develop a taste in reading or take a course in perhaps a special field you'd like to concentrate on.

Be prepared to be able to enjoy whatever life has in store for you, to find value in both the sunshine and the rain.

Strive For Inner Peace

Why is it that with all the pursuit of peace of mind, there still seems to be so much frustration and discontent? You can meditate and even achieve total communion with the entire universe, but how do you react when your radiator hose springs a leak?

I have nothing against meditation and similar practices. But I'm not at all certain that the method of working from the inside out is the most effective.

Some people advocate another method. "Act whatever it is you want to become. Act spiritual and you will become spiritual."

This method may not be quite as easy, but it is certainly likely to be more effective.

POSTSCRIPT

One of the collections of Charles Schulz' strips carries the title, "But We Love You, Charlie Brown."

Of course we love Charlie Brown. He is us.

There is some Charlie Brown in all of us. With some of us it is overt. With others it is disguised by various behavioral and psychological defense mechanisms, many of them operating on an unconscious level, that prevent the recognition of the Charlie Brown within ourselves. In either case, problems will arise.

If the reality is that we are more capable and likable than we consider ourselves to be, then our adjustment to the world is based on an inaccurate assessment of our capabilities, and that will cause trouble whether we are inveterate pessimists like Charlie Brown and precipitate our losses, or become overachievers in order to prove to ourselves as well as to everyone else that we are not the failures we think we are.

Sometimes we cannot accept success. In a recent television special, Charlie Brown was elected to escort the Homecoming Queen, who is none other than The Little Red-Haired Girl. Charlie Brown goes on to lose the game by missing a kick, but steals the show at the Homecoming Dance. He and The Little Red-Haired Girl are the life of the party, and they dance like no couple has ever danced before.

But, alas! The following day Charlie has a total amnesia about the dance. All he can remember is the disgrace and pain of missing the kick and losing the game.

What good is the stellar performance at the dance if he cannot recall it, if he has allowed his failure to overshadow his triumph? What good are our successes if we do not integrate them into our personality?

There is much we can do to make ourselves happier, but first we must recognize that some unhappiness is avoidable. Charlie Brown tells us about ourselves. If we listen and perceive, then we can look for ways to change things.

When Do The Good Things Start? They can start right now, but you must take the necessary steps to undo the distortion of your self-image. It is up to you to discover and believe the pleasant truth about yourself.